I0814085

SYMBOLS OF THE USA!

AMERICAN BISON

by Julie Murray

Cody Koala

An Imprint of Pop!

popbooksonline.com

Hello! My name is Cody Koala

This book is filled with videos, puzzles, games, and more! Scan the QR codes* while you read, or visit the website below to make this book pop.

popbooksonline.com/Bison

*Scanning QR codes requires a web-enabled smart device with a QR code reader app and a camera.

abdobooks.com

Published by Pop!, a division of ABDO, PO Box 398166, Minneapolis, Minnesota 55439. Copyright ©2026 by Abdo Consulting Group, Inc. International copyrights reserved in all countries. No part of this book may be reproduced in any form without written permission from the publisher. Cody Koala™ is a trademark and logo of Pop!.

Printed in the United States of America, North Mankato, Minnesota.

082025
012026

Cover Photo: Shutterstock Images
Interior Photos: Getty Images; Shutterstock Images
Editors: Elizabeth Andrews and Grace Hansen
Series Designer: Victoria Bates

Library of Congress Control Number: 2025940966

Publisher's Cataloging-in-Publication Data

Names: Murray, Julie, author.
Title: American Bison / by Julie Murray
Description: Minneapolis, Minnesota : Pop!, 2026 | Series: Symbols of the USA! | Includes online resources and index
Identifiers: ISBN 9781098248604 (lib. bdg.) | ISBN 9781098249120 (ebook)
Subjects: LCSH: American bison--Juvenile literature. | American buffalo--Juvenile literature. | National images--Juvenile literature. | Plains animals--Juvenile literature. | Signs and symbols--United States--Juvenile literature.
Classification: DDC 599.643--dc23

Table of Contents

Chapter 1
American Bison 4

Chapter 2
Large Numbers 6

Chapter 3
Facing Extinction 10

Chapter 4
Saving the Bison 12

Making Connections 22
Glossary 23
Index 24
Online Resources 24

Chapter 1

American Bison

American bison have lived in North America for more than 150,000 years. They are the largest land animal in the United States.

Bison stand 6 feet (1.8 m) tall. They weigh more than 2,000 pounds (907 kg)

Watch a video here!

Chapter 2

Large Numbers

In the early 1800s, 30 to 60 million bison lived in the US. They traveled across the country to find food. Herds of bison **grazed** the land and helped create rich soil.

A group of bison is called a herd.

Learn more here!

Where Do Bison Live?
North America
Original Bison Range
Bison Range After 1889
N
W
E
S

Bison were important to American Indians. They used bison for food, clothing, and shelter. Bison were also the center of **spiritual** life.

Chapter 3

Facing Extinction

By the late 1800s there were fewer than 1,000 bison left in the US. Illness and overhunting led to a large drop in bison numbers. European **settlers** were the main cause of overhunting.

Explore links here!

Chapter 4

Saving the Bison

People began trying to save the American bison. James "Scotty" Philip was a **rancher** in South Dakota. He helped grow bison numbers across the US.

James Philip

Complete an activity here!

In 1872, Yellowstone **National Park** opened. It was the world's first national park.

About 5,000 bison live in Yellowstone National Park.

Today, it is home to the largest herd of wild bison in the United States.

President Theodore Roosevelt started many national parks and other safe places for wildlife. He also passed laws that protected animals in these areas.

In 2016, The National Bison Legacy Act was passed. It named bison the national **mammal**.

Bison are honored for their place in history and as a **symbol** of the United States.

Today, about 500,000 bison live in the US. Most are found in state and national parks. They stand for **unity** and strength in America.

Bison can run up to 35 miles per hour (56 kph)!

Making Connections

Text-to-Self

Have you ever seen a bison? If so, where did you see it?

Text-to-Text

Have you read any other books about American symbols? If so, what were they and why are they important?

Text-to-World

Most bison live in state or national parks. Have you ever been to one of these parks? What animals did you see there?

Glossary

graze – to feed on plants.

mammal – a warm-blooded animal that produces milk for its young and is usually covered with hair.

national park – a large area cared for by a national government for public use and enjoyment.

rancher – someone who cares for animals on a large farm.

settler – a person who moves to a new area.

spiritual – having to do with people's beliefs in things, such as the soul, nature, and what happens after death.

symbol – an item or image that stands for something else.

unity – the condition of acting as one.

Index

appearance, 4

bison habits, 6

bison population, 6, 10, 15, 20

hunting, 10

importance, 9, 19–20

National Bison Legacy Act, 18

parks, 14, 17, 20

Philip, James "Scotty," 12

Roosevelt, Theodore, 17

Online Resources

popbooksonline.com

Thanks for reading this Cody Koala book!

This book is filled with videos, puzzles, games, and more! Scan the QR codes* while you read, or visit the website below to make this book pop.

popbooksonline.com/Bison

*Scanning QR codes requires a web-enabled smart device with a QR code reader app and a camera.